DIVING AND SNORKELING GUIDE TO

The Red Sea

John Ratterree

Pisces Books™
A division of Gulf Publishing Company
Houston, Texas

Publisher's note: At the time of publication of this book, all the information was determined to be as accurate as possible. However, when you use this guide, new construction may have changed land reference points, weather may have altered reef configurations, and some businesses may no longer be in operation. Your assistance in keeping future editions up-to-date will be greatly appreciated.

Also, please pay particular attention to the diver rating system in this book. Know your limits!

All photographs by John Ratterree except where otherwise noted.

Pisces Books
A division of Gulf Publishing Company
P.O. Box 2608, Houston, Texas 77252-2608

Library of Congress Cataloging-in-Publication Data

Ratterree, John.
Diving and snorkeling guide to the Red Sea / John Ratterree.
p. cm.
Includes index.
ISBN 1-55992-081-5
1. Deep diving—Red Sea—Guidebooks. 2. Skin diving—Red Sea—Guidebooks. 3. Red Sea—Guidebooks. I. Title.
GV840.S78R38 1995
797.2′3—dc20 94-25371
CIP

Printed in Hong Kong

10 9 8 7 6 5 4 3 2 1

Table of Contents

Preface

Since my first trip to the Red Sea in 1979, I have witnessed the staggering growth of the diving industry in Sharm El Sheikh and Na'ama Bay. At times, there are now more than 1,000 divers in this area at any given time. Fortunately the Egyptian Environmental Affairs Agency foresaw problems from this type of growth and in 1983, Ras Muhammed National Park was declared protected by Law 102 of 1983. This law clearly defined the activities that could be carried out within this protected area.

The area included in the Ras Muhammed National Park begins at the Gulf of Suez and extends north to include all of Sharm El Sheikh, Na'ama Bay, the Straights of Tiran, and all of the islands in the Straights. The rules of mooring and the number of divers in any given location at any given time is strictly controlled. These rules have lessened the impact of the increasing numbers of divers in any one area.

My congratulations to the Egyptian Government for taking these steps and for their ongoing work in protecting one of the greatest diving areas of the world.

John Ratterree

How To Use This Guide

This guide will familiarize you with the most popular and unique dive sites of the Red Sea. Most of the diving in this area is done with a shore-based, day boat dive operation or from a liveaboard dive boat. Thus you will not have to locate the dive areas yourself and a dive operator will brief you on what to expect underwater. Most of the dive sites listed here can only be reached with a boat and local guide. The currents in all these areas can vary from none to very extreme, so it is best to dive and snorkel with guides or experienced divers who are familiar with the conditions of the area.

A curious humphead wrasse looks over the divers at the Near Garden dive site. (Photo: Esther Ratterree)

The Rating System for Divers and Dive Sites

Before you enter the water for any dive, you should consider the following: how you feel that particular day, your general physical condition, the weather and water conditions, and your level of training to deal with *all* of these items. Although you may have traveled a great distance at great expense, don't let one dive ruin the whole trip or, even worse, risk your life on a dive you do not feel right about. Be honest about evaluating your diving skills.

A *snorkeler* is someone who is a good swimmer and is skilled in ocean snorkeling. A *novice diver* is someone in good physical condition who has recently completed a basic certification diving course, or a certified diver who has not been diving recently or who has no experience in similar waters. An *advanced diver* is someone who has experienced (logged) many dives under similar or rougher conditions and is in good physical condition. A *dive master or instructor* is someone with advanced training as a dive master, or an instructor who has logged over 100 dives under similar conditions and is in excellent physical condition.

Buoyancy control is essential while drift diving the reefs. Here a diver adjusts his buoyancy on a drift dive at Shark Bay. (Photo: Esther Ratterree)

Because most divers who travel to destinations such as the Red Sea engage in underwater photography and underwater videography as part of their normal diving activities, they must consider this in the evaluation of their diving skills. Only after you become comfortable underwater, can you concentrate on photography or videography. Buoyancy control is essential. Maintaining neutral buoyancy will allow you to hold your position in midwater, hover off the bottom, and glide smoothly through the water. Once you can do this effortlessly and without having to kick furiously to stay in place, you will be ready to practice camera handling and be successful in underwater photography and videography. Proper buoyancy control is a must in the Red Sea for protection of the marine environment, and guides will bar you from the water if you are caught destroying coral, even inadvertently with your fins.

Liveaboard dive boats at their night moorings off Sanafir Island in the Straights of Tiran. (Photo: Robert Stribling)

Dive Site Ratings

	Snorkeler	Novice w/Instructor	Advanced	Dive Master or Instructor
Aqaba, Jordan				
1 Southern Section	X	X	X	X
2 Fara'un Island	X	X	X	X
Eilat, Israel				
3 Eilat Coastline	X	X	X	X
Sharm el Sheikh, Egypt				
4 Near Garden	X	X	X	X
5 Far Garden	X	X	X	X
6 Shark Bay		X	X	X
7 White Night	X	X	X	X
8 Ras Nasrani	X	X	X	X
9 Gordon Reef		X	X	X
10 Jackson Reef		X	X	X
11 Coral Garden (Hushasha)		X	X	X
12 Koshkasha		X	X	X
13 Abu Tinun		X	X	X
14 Sinafar Island		X	X	X
15 Flasher Reef		X	X	X
16 Tower		X	X	X
17 Ras Um Sid	X	X	X	X
18 Temple		X	X	X
19 Ras Za'atir		X	X	X
20 Fisherman's Banks	X	X	X	X
21 Ras Mohammed (Shark Reef)	X	X	X	X
22 Alternatives		X	X	X
23 Beacon Rock (*Dunraven Wreck*)			X	X
24 Sha'ab Ali (*Thistlegorm Wreck*)			X	X
25 Gubal Island		X	X	X
26 Abu Nuhas (Ships' Graveyard)			X	X
27 El-Akhawein (The Brothers)				X
Sudan Coast				
28 Sha'ab Su'adi (Toyota Wreck)				X
29 Sha'ab Roumi				X
30 Sanganeb				X
31 Wingate Reef (*Umbria Wreck*)				X
Dahlak Islands, Eritrea				
32 Dahlak Islands				X

1

Overview of the Red Sea

The Red Sea encompasses a large area beginning in the south at the narrow straights between the countries of Djibouti and Yemen. It then extends north to the tip of the Sinai, where it splits into the Gulf of Suez and the Gulf of Aqaba.

This body of water borders many nations and more than a hundred individually known dive sites. Of these nations only three currently provide for easily accessible tourism and diving on their shores. These nations are Egypt, Israel, and Jordan. While Jordan and Israel have only small areas at the very end of the Gulf of Eilat/Aqaba, most of the diving and snorkeling sites are within the boundaries of, or under the dominion of, Egypt.

All three of these nations not only offer magnificent diving and snorkeling, but an additional feature as well. This added feature is the opportunity to conduct side visits (extensions) to some of the most famous and amazing ancient archaeological sites in the world. Some of these extensions may require as much time to visit as does the diving.

The entrance to the 10th-century city of Petra, in Jordan. This building is called the Treasury and was filmed for the movie Indiana Jones and the Last Crusade.

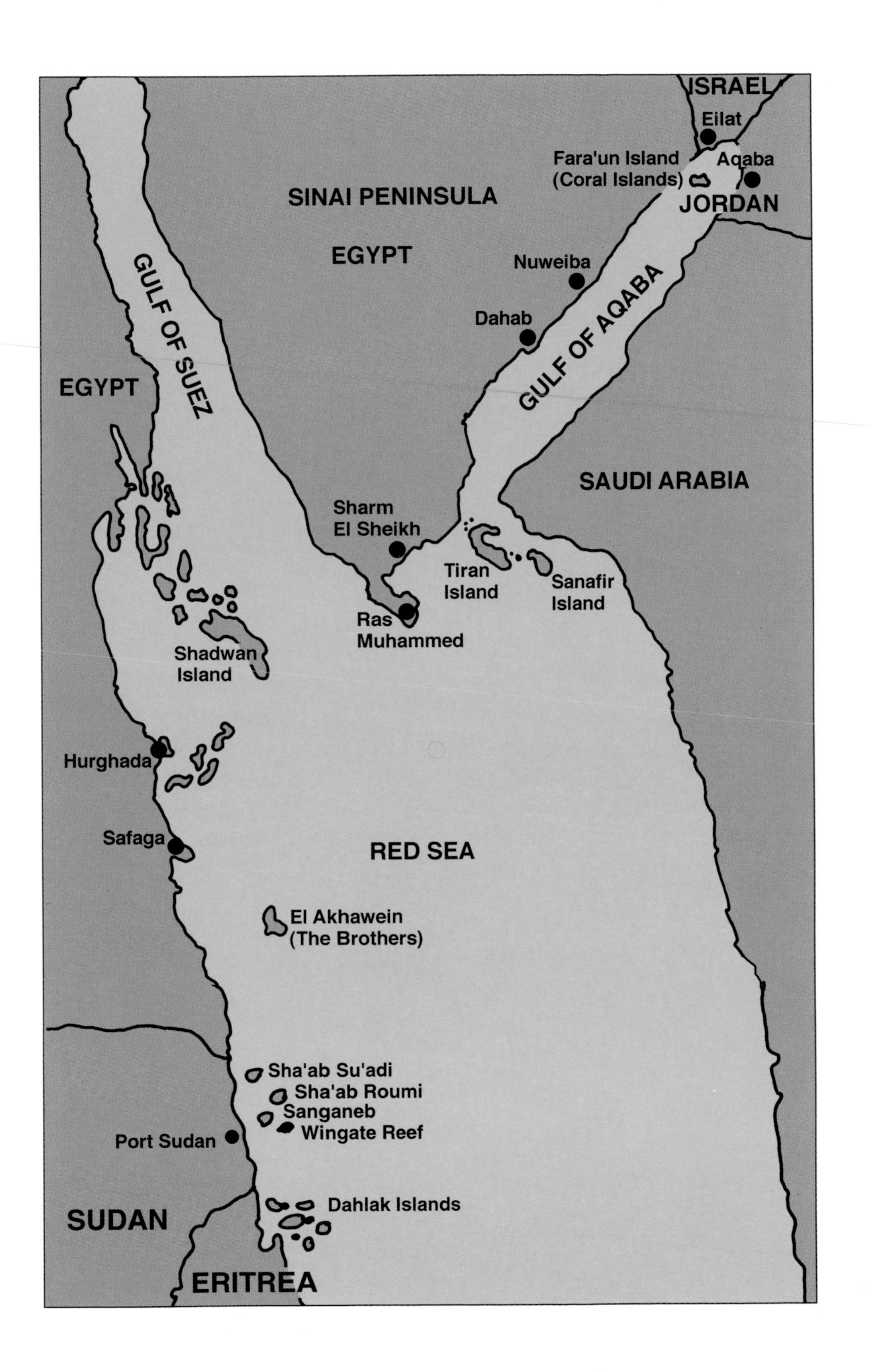
ISRAEL
Eilat
Fara'un Island
(Coral Islands)
Aqaba
JORDAN
SINAI PENINSULA
EGYPT
Nuweiba
Dahab
GULF OF SUEZ
GULF OF AQABA
EGYPT
SAUDI ARABIA
Sharm
El Sheikh
Tiran
Island
Sanafir
Island
Ras
Muhammed
Shadwan
Island
Hurghada
Safaga
RED SEA
El Akhawein
(The Brothers)
Sha'ab Su'adi
Sha'ab Roumi
Sanganeb
Wingate Reef
Port Sudan
Dahlak Islands
SUDAN
ERITREA

Jordan

Jordan occupies a section of shoreline at the upper most corner of the Gulf of Aqaba. This shoreline stretches from its border with Saudi Arabia on the east to the border with Israel on the west. There are many accessible beaches along this shoreline, and this is where most of the resort/diving hotels are found.

Besides the diving, you should not miss the opportunity to visit the hidden city of Petra. You can visit Petra by organized tour or on your own by rental car, as it is only a two-hour drive from Aqaba. You may also like to visit Wadi Rum, a desert canyon near Aqaba.

Although these may not be everyday names to you, Petra was the Valley of the Crescent Moon in the movie *Indiana Jones and the Last Crusade,* and the desert canyons of Wadi Rum were the locations where most of *Lawrence of Arabia* was filmed.

Getting There: There are many flights to Amman, Jordan. From Amman, you then must take a one-hour flight to Aqaba. There are also some direct flights from some cities in Europe to Aqaba. You can also reach Aqaba by ferry from several ports in Egypt, which also serves many resort areas of that country as well.

Where to Stay: The major dive operators in Jordan operate out of hotels located on the beach in the city of Aqaba. These hotels vary from moderate to very expensive, depending on the level of comfort you want. Aqaba is a very clean city, and the hotels, whether they are cheap or expensive, reflect the cleanliness of the rest of the city.

Customs and Immigration: A valid passport is required as well as a visa, which can be obtained at the airport upon arrival. You must also possess a return ticket, and entry will be allowed for tourism only.

Currency: The currency in Jordan is the Jordanian dinar. U.S. currency and major credit cards are accepted at most of the hotels and resorts.

Israel

The area of Eilat, Israel is a section of shoreline at the uppermost western corner of the Gulf of Aqaba. This shoreline stretches from its border with Egypt on the west to the border with Jordan on the east. There are many accessible beaches along this shoreline. Most of the diving operations and dive resorts are located in the city of Eilat.

◄ *A look down "Main Street" in Petra from the ruins of a Roman-built coliseum.*

A view of the City of Jerusalem from a lookout on the Mount of Olives. (Photo: Robert Stribling)

While in Israel, you should not miss the opportunity to visit famous areas and sites such as the city of Jerusalem, Masada, the Dead Sea, and Jericho. You can visit these by organized tour or you can rent a car (be sure to get a map).

Getting There: There are many flights to Tel Aviv. From there you then must take a one-hour flight to Eilat. There are also some direct flights from some cities in Europe to Eilat. You can also reach Eilat by bus or by driving from Cairo/Sharm El Sheikh through the Sinai Peninsula in Egypt, although it can be a tiresome hassle at Taba, the Egypt/Israeli border in the Sinai.

Where to stay: The major dive operators in the Eilat area are in the city of Eilat proper. The hotels in Eilat vary from inexpensive to very expensive, depending on the level of comfort you desire. There is a considerable number of other vacation activities offered in Eilat beside diving, as well as night life for those so inclined. Besides hotels, many liveaboard dive boats operate out of Eilat, which is the point of embarkation and debarkation for these boats.

The Dome of the Rock (Mosque of Omar) is one of Islam's most sacred shrines and is located within the walls of the Old City of Jerusalem. (Photo: Robert Stribling) ►

When you visit Masada you not only get to enjoy the city, but you get a terrific view of the Dead Sea. (Photo: Robert Stribling)

Customs and Immigration: A valid passport is required as well as a visa that can be obtained at the airport upon arrival. You must also possess a return ticket, and entry will be allowed for tourism only.

Currency: The currency in Israel is the shekel. U.S. currency and major credit cards are accepted at most of the hotels and resorts.

◄ At the Dead Sea, you may want to coat yourself with stinky mud and jump in the highly salted water and float around like a cork. Then again, you may not! (Photo: Robert Stribling)

The beaches of Na'ama Bay, Sharm El Sheikh offer a wide range of water sports, but here diving is the main attraction. ►

> ***Bringing Cameras into the Area***
>
> Jordan, Israel, and Egypt are serious about their regulations for bringing video equipment and some still camera equipment into their respective countries. The customs officials will want to see all video recorders, cameras, and camcorders. Serial numbers of these items will be recorded in your passport, next to the visa for that country. Your passport will again be checked upon departure and you must make sure you are still in possession of *all* listed equipment. Keep this in mind when you pack so you can readily reach your equipment.

Egypt

Egypt has the largest easily accessible shoreline and includes most of the western shore of the Gulf of Aqaba. This area also includes all of the Gulf of Suez and the western shore of the Red Sea as far south as its border with Sudan. In addition, Egypt has jurisdictional rights to most of the islands in this area of the Red Sea. At present, Saudi Arabia prohibits diving tourism, and diving facilities are nonexistent in Sudan, Eritrea, Djibouti, and Yemen, which are the other countries that border the Red Sea. There are a few live-aboard boat dive operations that visit the southern areas of the Red Sea from time to time. These operations are allowed at the whims of the governments whose shorelines and territorial waters these boats operate in.

Huge statues mark the entrance to Western Thebes and the Valleys of the Kings and Queens.

In Egypt, most of the serious diving is from Sharm El Sheikh, with large resorts at Na'ama Bay. Many liveaboard dive boats operate from there. Hurghada and Safaga on the west shore of the Red Sea also boast of many resorts and liveaboard dive boats as well as excellent snorkeling and every conceivable water sport that can be imagined.

Egypt has some of the best-known antiquities in the world. After all, what would a trip to this area be without a visit to the Great Pyramids, Sakkara, Aswan (Abu Simbel), and Luxor with the Valley of the Kings and Queens and the Karnak Temple?

Getting There: There are many flights to Cairo, Hurghada, and Sharm El Sheikh from all over the world. Most transit through Europe and terminate in Cairo. There are many flights daily from Cairo to Sharm El Sheikh, Hurghada, Safaga, and Aqaba. There is also good air-conditioned bus service from Cairo to Na'ama Bay (Sharm El Sheikh) daily at very low cost.

Where to stay: Every level of accommodations is available from facilities for camper vans to ultra luxury suites at large hotels and a few small villas that can be rented or leased.

Large statues and pillars dwarf the photographer at Luxor Temple. This is one of the many sites open to you when you experience a Nile Cruise from Aawan to Luxor. ▶

Full Visa Needed for Ras Mohammed National Park

You must obtain a full tourist visa before arrival in Egypt if you want to dive in Ras Mohammed National Park. Travel agents will tell you you can obtain a visa at the airport upon arrival in Egypt. While this is true, the visa you obtain at the airport is a mini visa and not a full tourist visa with applicable tax stamps. If you fail to obtain the full visa before arrival in Egypt, *YOU WILL NOT BE ABLE TO DIVE IN RAS MOHAMMED NATIONAL PARK.* On a recent trip to Sharm El Sheikh, I counted 20 divers from many different nations who had only mini visas obtained at the airport upon arrival, and these divers were not allowed to join us on day trips to Ras Mohammed. This occurred in four days with only one dive operation. You can imagine the total number of divers who make this mistake every year. By the way, there is no way to obtain the full visa while in Egypt.

Customs and Immigration: A valid passport is required, and a visa must be obtained from the nearest Egyptian Consulate before departure for Egypt. You must also possess a return ticket, and entry will be allowed for tourism only. Your passport with the valid visa must be stamped every seven days during your stay in Egypt. This is usually handled at your hotel desk or by your dive operator.

Currency: The currency in Egypt is the Egyptian pound LE. U.S. currency and major credit cards are accepted at most of the hotels, resorts, and dive operations.

◀ A great way to relax during the hectic tour of temples is to go on a Fluka Sail on the Nile below the Aswan Dam.

Pages from an early snorkeling guide to the Red Sea are found on the wall of an Egyptian temple along the Nile. Egyptians are rumored to have used papyrus reeds as snorkels. (Photo: Robert Stribling)▶

Sudan and Eritrea

Recent and ongoing political tensions in these areas make most land-based diving operations tenuous, if not impossible, on a regular bases; thus, most of the diving access in this region is by liveaboard boat operations only.

As with all dive sites in this part of the Red Sea, this area can be most safely accessed during very good weather conditions, because there are no land masses for protection. Any high winds or wave conditions can be extremely dangerous for mooring and diving activities.

Naturally, because of the hazards of this region, it has to be one of the most beautiful areas of the Red Sea and offers divers an incredible variety of marine life. Again, I must reiterate however, this area comes at a high cost in travel difficulties and adverse conditions.

Getting There: Most of the liveaboard boat operations operate out of Eilat, Sharm El Sheikh, and the southern Egyptian ports of Hurghada and Safaga; thus, getting to these areas is easy. If you must board or disembark in one of the other nations in this region, you have my sympathy and best wishes.

Where to Stay: Again this region is best accessed by liveaboard boat operations; thus, all accommodations are included in this operation.

Customs and Immigration: You are required to have a valid passport at your disposal at all times while traveling in this region. If you will be boarding or disembarking in one of the nations in the southern Red Sea, you must check with that nation about visa requirements and documentation required no matter how short your visit. This of course must be done prior to your arrival in that nation because, in most cases, it is not possible once you arrive.

◀ *When you visit the Egyptian Museum in Cairo, if you choose to pay a small fee you can bring your cameras into the museum and take photos like this one of Tutankhamun's burial mask.*

2

Diving in Jordan and Israel

Where the Gulf of Aqaba ends, it forms a crescent-shaped area made up of a continuous beach that extends through the countries of Jordan and Israel. The border between these two countries extends from the Gulf of Aqaba up a dry wash to the Dead Sea to the north. It is apparent from looking at this wash that the Gulf and the Dead Sea were once connected.

At present, crossing the border at Eilat/Aqaba is not possible. However, you can take the ferry from Aqaba to Nuweiba into Egypt, drive north along the Sinai, and cross the border at Taba into Israel. This is not an easy task, but it can be done if you are determined to do so.

The diving in this area of the Gulf is different from that of Sharm El Sheikh. There is little current and many shallow areas that allow for large meadows, which provide breeding grounds as well as feeding areas for many animals. The climate is hot and dry because of the surrounding deserts, with average air temperatures around 90°F (32°C) in summer and 65°F (18°C) in winter. Rainfall averages less than 1 inch (22 mm) annually. Strong winds blow year round, with most of them blowing north to south, carrying desert sands with them. The deep bottom sediments are therefore mostly of desert origin.

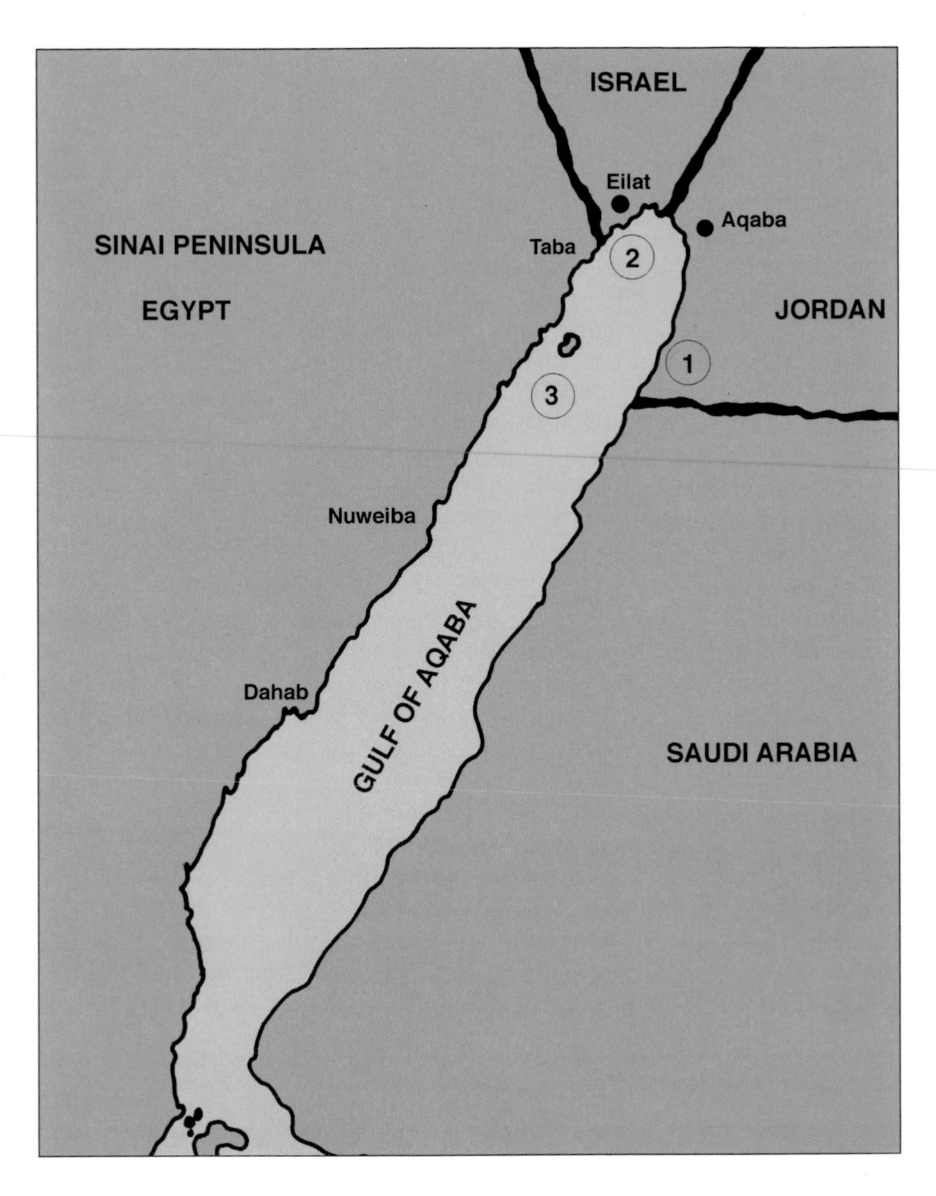

The Gulf waters are colder than those to the south at Sharm El Sheikh because of the intense evaporation. At depths below 650 feet (200 meters) the temperature is a constant 70°F (21°C), while at the surface the annual change is only from about 65°F (18°C) to 79°F (26°C). The water in the Gulf is also highly concentrated. Normal seawater is made up of approximately 3.5% salts throughout most of the world. The salts in the Gulf of Aqaba make up 4.1% to 4.3% of the seawater solution.

◀ *An aerial view of the North End of the Gulf of Aqaba. The City of Aqaba Jordan is at the bottom, and the City of Eilat, Israel is in the distance at the top.*

Jordan's Southern Section 1

Location:	Jordan's southern coast
Attractions:	Corals, lionfish, eels, cuttlefish, turtles and sharks
Typical depth range:	20–120 feet (6–37 meters)
Access:	Shore dive, boat dive, local guide
Expertise required:	Snorkeler to advanced

Jordan's coastline extends from its border with Israel at the extreme northern end of the Gulf for a distance of 16.8 miles (27 km) down the eastern shore. Although this distance is short, it contains considerable underwater features, and is rich in marine life.

The northern end of the Gulf is made up of a continuous sandy shoreline with a few patches of stone. This shoreline gradually slopes underwater with many sea grass meadows. Most of the hotels and diving resorts are located along this stretch of shoreline, but the best diving is found to the south.

The Port of Aqaba occupies the next section of the shoreline, but here dredging and other construction activities have caused considerable destruction of the marine environment. Steps are being taken to help restore this area, and a few adaptable species have flourished.

South of the port, the coastal mountains extend to the shore and continue underwater as steep submarine cliffs. These dropoffs are home to many corals, fan corals, and whip corals that grow off the walls of the cliff face. Many pelagic deep-water animals can be seen swimming through this area.

The most southern coastal area to the border with Saudi Arabia is a series of promontories and bays. Here the prevailing winds drive waves and currents parallel to the coast. Around each bay the north-facing beaches are exposed to waves, while the south-facing beaches are more protected. Parallel to this shore is a fringing coral reef that is met by the sloping sandy bottom at 60 feet (18 meters). The massive coral structure of this reef with

A white moray eel comes out of its hole to search the sea grasses for food. There is an abundance of marine animals to be found in these grasses in Aqaba's dive sites.

tunnels, crevices, and different surfaces, forms a rich and productive habitat for thousands of marine species.

The main attractions are in the sea grass area from 15 feet to 45 feet (4.6 to 14 meters) where you will find many eels, cuttlefish, sea horses, and stingrays. Then moving down the sand, you will find many garden eels and sea pens, until you reach the reef with its hard corals, soft corals, fan corals, lionfish, white moray eels, clown anemonefish, and all the other fish and animals the Red Sea is noted for.

Some areas have names such as the Coral Gardens, The Ladder, and The Wreck, which is a derelict freighter that sank there in shallow water about ten years ago. A local guide is required even for shore diving in Jordan. The names of some of these sites change per any given guide. Because all the good dive sites are located in a small area, they all are similar and offer excellent diving and snorkeling.

◀ While swimming over the grasses at the coral gardens dive site, you may encounter one of these beautiful cuttlefish to photograph or video.

Soft corals grow from a man-made structure, at the wreck dive site in Aqaba. ▼

Fara'un Island (Coral Island) 2

Location: Gulf of Aqaba
Attractions: Wall, corals, lionfish, and reef fish
Typical depth range: 10–160 feet (3–49 meters)
Access: Boat dive, local guide
Expertise required: Snorkeler to instructor

The Fara'un Island lies offshore from Egypt's Sinai Peninsula across from Jordan's Port of Aqaba. It is accessible from Jordan and by boat from the Sinai mainland. As you approach the island, it appears to be a very large Citadel floating on the Gulf. This is because the Citadel occupies most of the island's area except the lagoon area where you can dock and go ashore.

While the lagoon area is great for snorkeling, the best diving is on the seaward side and is a steep wall dropoff starting at 10 feet (3 meters) and dropping to a shelf at 160 feet (49 meters). The bottom then continues down to great depths in the Gulf, and many pelagic, sharks, rays, jacks, and turtles swim by from time to time.

The Citadel on Fara'un Island appears to rise from the sea when you approach the island by boat.

A view of Fara'un Island from the Sinai mainland. (Photo: Robert Stribling)

Fara'un Island

Fara'un Island is a protected area of Egypt and subject to regulations for its use. You must pay a fee for day use and are required to present your passport to the park office for entry. If you enter by boat, this will be handled by the dive operation, but you must have your passport with you always. The purchase of a waterproof container for your passport is a good investment because you are required to have your passport on your person at all times throughout most of the Middle East.

Besides the pelagic animals, some of the attractions in this area are soft corals, hard corals, fan corals, clown anemonefish, and an over abundance of lionfish. These lionfish are out feeding most times of the day, and seem to be waiting for any diver wanting to view or photograph them.

Eilat, Israel Coastline 3

Location:	Gulf of Aqaba
Attractions:	Sandy sloping bottom with many coral heads and fish
Typical depth range:	20–120 feet (6–37 meters)
Access:	Shore dive, boat dive, local guide
Expertise required:	Snorkeler to Advanced

The northern end of the Gulf is made up of continuous sandy shoreline with a few patches of stone. This gradually slopes underwater with many sea grass meadows. Most of the hotels and diving resorts are located along this stretch of shoreline, and the best diving is found to the south.

The Port of Eilat occupies a good section of Eilat's small shoreline, which tends to limit diving access. However, there are many day boat and liveaboard dive boat operators based in Eilat, who can provide you with access and can transport you to the best diving areas along the Eilat coastline and on into the Gulf of Aqaba and beyond.

◀ *A lionfish swims in shallow water to feed along the wall of the Fara'un Island dive site.*

The undulate triggerfish is one of the colorful reef fishes found on the coral heads and walls in the Eilat diving area. (Photo: Robert Stribling)

Here shore diving takes place in a gradually sloping sandy bottom with sea grass patches that are home to cuttlefish, sea horses, eels, and sting rays. Coral heads can also be found that are home to invertebrates (corals, nudibrachs, and flat worms), many varieties of fish, and even an octopus or two.

Boat diving with local guides includes coral reefs and wall diving along the south coast. Here many fish swim by the corals on the walls. This coast extends to the border with Egypt at Taba to the south and territorial waters out into approximately the middle of the Gulf.

There are plenty of other water sports to enjoy in Eilat, such as water skiing, para-sailing, jet skiing, and just plain swimming. A visit to the aquarium in Eilat will provide a diver with a good idea of what to look for in the Gulf when diving or snorkeling.

Soft corals are found in many colors on coral heads and walls at many of Eilat's dive sites. ►

This longnose hawkfish has moved from the fan coral it normally frequents to pose for the photographer. (Photo: Robert Stribling)

3

Diving in Sharm El Sheikh, Egypt, Sudan and Eritrea

All snorkeling and diving activities in the Sharm El Sheikh area are within the boundaries of the Sinai National Park. Dive sites 4 through 23 are located within the park and subject to all of the regulations that apply according to the terms of Law 102, 1983. These regulations are posted at all major dive operations and are available from the park office. The following are the main points of the regulations to keep in mind for all areas of the Park:

- Dive in designated diving areas only. Do not walk or anchor on the reefs.
- Fishing and spearfishing are prohibited, as is the removal or damage of any material, living or dead (such as coral, shells, fish, plants, fossils) from the park.

The diving in the Sharm El Sheikh area is spectacular, with many walls, drift dives in the currents, and the intense color of the underwater marine life that is such a stark contrast to the monotone arid desert that surrounds

The deep blue waters of the Gulf of Aqaba come right up to the barren rugged shore line of the Sinai Peninsula. This stark contrast goes even further when you see the vivid colors awaiting just under the surface of these waters. (Photo: Robert Stribling)

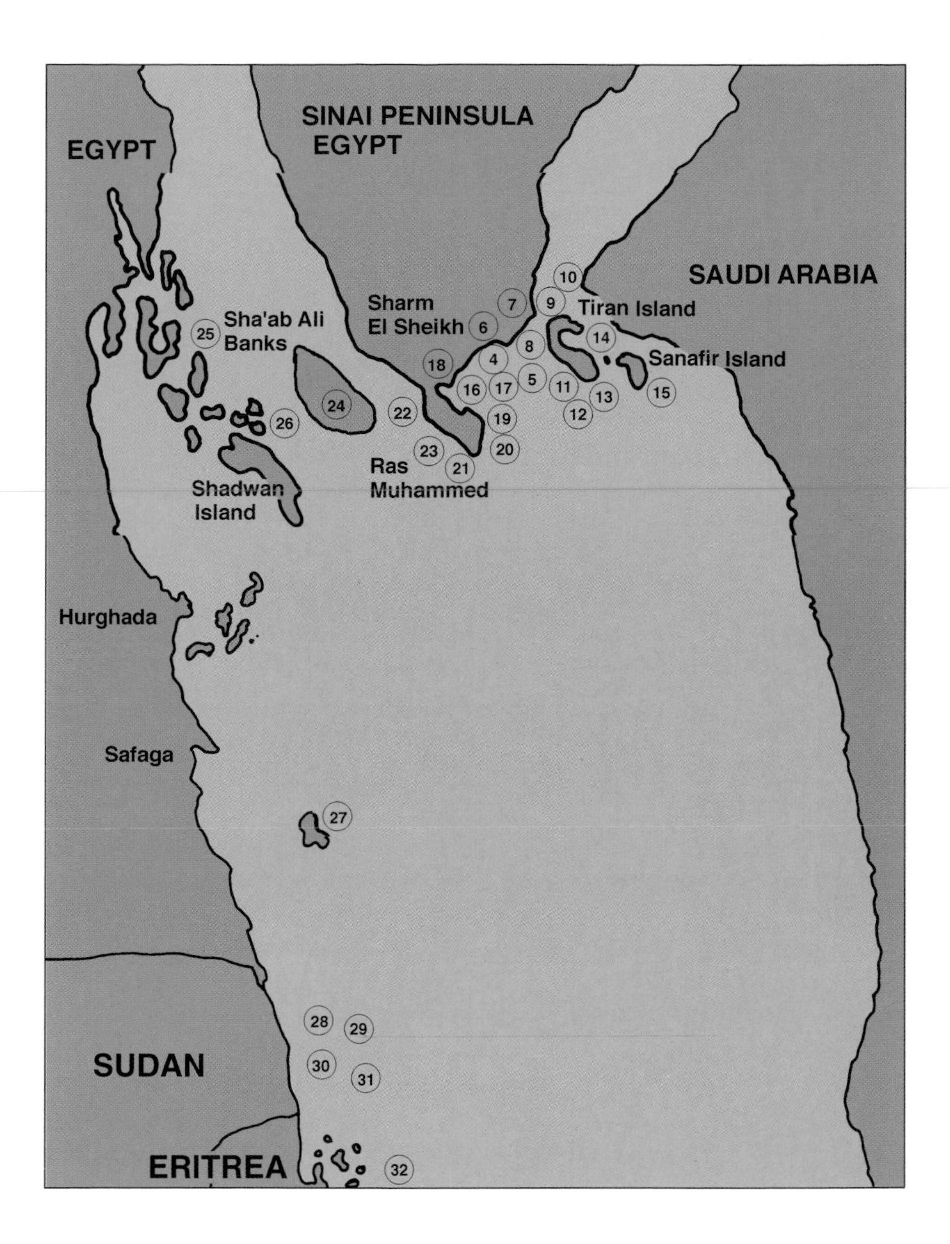

it. The climate is hot and dry as a result of the surrounding deserts, with average air temperatures around 130°F (55°C) in summer and 78°F (26°C) in winter. Rainfall averages less than 1 inch (22 mm) annually.

The waters are warmer than those in the Gulf to the north, and at the surface the annual change is from about 75°F (24°C) to 82°F (28°C). Like the water in the Gulf, the water here is also highly concentrated. It contains approximately 20% greater salt concentration than the normal seawater found in most oceans of the world.

Near Garden 4

Location:	North entrance to Na'ama Bay
Attractions:	Shallow wall with sloped drop off
Typical depth range:	5–100 feet (2–30 meters)
Access:	Shore dive, boat dive, local guide
Expertise required:	Snorkeler novice to advanced

The Near Garden is a coral shelf extending out from the shore at the north point of Na'ama Bay. It extends at a shallow depth for about 20 feet (6 meters) then slopes off to 100 feet (30 meters) to a sandy bottom. Along the slope you will find sand channels rising to the coral shelf in some places.

The sloping wall is covered with hard corals, fan corals and soft corals, making colorful homes for many fish species. There are some large resident humphead wrasses, which will sometimes frighten you by swimming up

Yellowband or map angelfish as it is better known is found only in the Red Sea area. It is called the map angelfish because the yellow band on its side resembles a map of the Sinai Peninsula.

◀ Here, just below the surface at Ras Nasrani is an example of the vivid color that abounds in the Red Sea.

along side or above you in hopes of getting a handout of food. Feeding of fish by divers is prohibited because it upsets the biological balance on the reef. Some divers disregard this regulation, and some of the fish have grown accustomed to the handouts. The area is also used by glass-bottom boat tours and snorkel tours, so a lot of fish feeding goes on here in defiance of the law. This does have a side benefit to divers in that it attracts a large number of tropical fish, and they are easily approachable for photography and videography.

Because of its location in Na'ama Bay, the Near Garden is an excellent location for night dives for land-based dive operations. There is no disappointment because of this close proximity, and it is truly a great night dive location. The reef changes completely at night, with the feather and basket stars coming out to feed in the currents. The combination of no sunlight and the use of dive lights enhances the entire reef, covering it with color from the soft corals and sponges that abound.

During the dive, the dive boat will attach to the provided mooring and diving will start at the mooring line and end there as well. The best plan is to proceed against the current (if there is one) at the start of the dive, and return with the current to the boat and mooring at the end of the dive.

Although the Near Garden dive site is close to the resorts at Na'ama Bay, it does not want for any color or diversity in its reef or the animals that are found here. (Photo: Esther Ratterree) ▶

The color at Near Garden is made up of many reef fishes like this colorful coral grouper.

Far Garden 5

Location:	North of Na'ama Bay
Attractions:	Deep wall with steep dropoff, shallow caves and large overhangs
Typical depth range:	10–165 feet (3–50 meters)
Access:	Shore dive, boat dive, local guide
Expertise required:	Snorkeler, novice to advanced

The Far Garden is a coral wall that drops off from the shore and continues to a depth 160 feet (50 meters) to the bottom. Along the wall, you will find caves in the shallow areas 20 to 40 feet (6 to 12 meters). These caves contain schools of glass sweeper fish, and on night dives the famous flashlight fish can sometimes be found here. Large overhangs are found in the deeper areas 100–120 feet (30 to 37 meters). These are covered with large fan corals, soft corals, and even a few black coral trees still exist here.

Fan corals cover an opening in a coral head as if they were curtains for a stage at the Far Garden. ▶

Humphead wrasses are found along the Shram El Sheikh coast and seem to be very curious about the divers or perhaps they are just looking for a handout. (Photo: Esther Ratterree)

As with the Near Garden, this site is popular for night dives with the land-based day boat operators. You leave at dusk (5:00 p.m. or 17:00 hours), and it is dark when you enter the water. The reef really comes alive at night, and you cannot believe it is the same place you dived in the day light. Be sure to turn off your dive light from time to time, and you may be lucky enough to witness the spots of light swimming back and forth. These flashlight fish are truly a joy to watch and will come close if you have the patience to wait.

◀ A sandy shelf at the Far Garden is the domain of this bluespotted grouper.

One of many lionfish at the Far Garden hovers around a colorful soft coral. ▼

Shark Bay 6

Location:	A small bay north of Na'ama Bay
Attractions:	Canyon with a wall
Typical depth range:	30–85 feet (10–26 meters)
Access:	Boat dive, local guide
Expertise required:	Novice to advanced

Shark Bay consists of a bay formed by the rugged shoreline dropping down below the surface to a sandy canyon bottom. This bottom then slopes down to a wall that drops to 85 feet (26 meters). The wall that drops from the shore is made up of crevices that contain many soft corals and numerous small red fish that move continuously and provide a cover for the reef. Some divers have contended that these small red fish (lyretail coralfish) are the reason divers call this area the Red Sea. While you concentrate on the reef, you may want to look out in the blue water from time to time. You just may glimpse a spotted eagle ray, a great barracuda or, of course, what the bay was named for—a shark.

The dive site may be called Shark Bay, but this barracuda silhouettes itself between the sun and the camera. Maybe it doesn't know the name.

White Night 7

Location: Inside the point of Ras Nasrani
Attractions: Sloping wall with sand splits and large coral heads
Typical depth range: 10–85 feet (3–26 meters)
Access: Shore dive, boat dive, local guide
Expertise required: Snorkeler, novice to advanced

White Night starts from the shore as a small wall descending to 20 feet (6 meters). It then becomes a sandy slope with large boulders and coral heads. These boulders and coral heads are very prolific with animal life including fan corals, hard corals, and many soft corals. Many large groupers and a few humphead wrasses may be found observing divers on the wall.

While exploring these coral heads and boulders, pay close attention to the coral because you may spot a scorpion fish or two well-camouflaged with the background. You really do not want to find these fish by touch. Their dorsal spines are very toxic, so it is best to find them by observation.

Soft corals grow over the edge on a wall as they drop over into the depths below. (Photo: Esther Ratterree) ▶

Easy shore access makes White Night a great place for snorkeling as well as diving.

Ras Nasrani 8

Location:	At the start of the Straights of Tiran
Attractions:	Steep dropoff, large pelagic fish
Typical depth range:	30–130 feet (10–40 meters)
Access:	Drift dive, boat dive, local guide
Expertise required:	Advanced to dive master/instructor

As the White Night dive site continues to the point, it becomes Ras Nasrani. The point of Ras Nasrani has strong currents most of the time and is usually a drift dive. The boat will usually start you out up-current. You will then drift with the current, and the boat will be with you at the end of the dive.

The large fan corals grow between the outcroppings and the coral wall creating canyons with what appears to be curtains at the entrance. There will usually be many soft corals on these outcroppings, and they become a very colorful site with the fans and fish that frequent them.

A well-camouflaged stonefish is very hard to find against the coral background at Ras Nasrani.

Drift Diving

Drift diving is a necessity in many parts of the Red Sea. Because of the tide changes and the waters passing through small straights during these tide changes, very strong currents develop. These currents make mooring dives almost impossible in some areas. These currents become a mode of transportation for experienced divers as they propel them through the water with ease. This reduces the amount of effort required, and saves energy, air, and prolongs the dive. It can also be a lot of fun because it is a free ride. Buoyancy control is essential, and because there can be up and down currents as well, a constant awareness of your computer and adjustments to your buoyancy compensator is a good way to stay out of trouble.

When trying to take still photos or to observe a static subject, there is a tendency to latch onto the reef, hold tight, and stop your motion. This procedure can be detrimental to the reef as well as to you. It can result in broken coral, displaced animals, and cuts and bruises to your body.

Always pay attention to your guide's pre-dive briefing. Follow the guide's instructions, and under strong current conditions, stick with the guide on drift dives if you are not familiar with the site.

Some type of locating device, such as a safety sausage or strobe light at night is a must. Some operators, such as *Sinai Divers,* give all divers who do not have a device a long, narrow, bright yellow plastic bag to inflate with their safe second or primary regulators. The diver twists the end of the bag tightly and pulls it under water until the bar sticks straight upright about 3 feet (1 meter) above the water. This device helps the boat operator locate a diver who may have gotten caught in a strong current and pulled away from the group.

There are many pelagic fish that swim through here on their way in and out of the Straights of Tiran. These include many sharks, including schools of young sharks feeding on bait fish near the surface. Also there are many jacks, tuna, and barracuda to be found here. On occasion, large turtles are seen slowly moving on their way along the reef, and seem to have a look at divers as they pass.

There are many ways to enjoy a drift dive, as here where a diver has chosen to ride his dive cylinder instead of wearing it.

A beautiful lionfish glides along with full plumage out over the colorful coral at Ras Nasrani.

Gordon Reef 9

Location: In the Straights of Tiran
Attractions: Sloping wall, strong currents and large pelagic fish
Typical depth range: 10–225 feet (10–70 meters)
Access: Drift dive, boat dive, local guide
Expertise required: Novice with instructor, advanced to dive master/instructor

Gordon Reef is a coral reef that rises from the bottom to just below the surface of the water at high tide. This reef is in the middle of the Straights of Tiran, between the Sinai mainland and Tiran island. The area between it and the Sinai mainland is the main shipping channel on the western side of the Straights. This channel is very deep and comes up very fast to Gordon Reef. Because this reef is such a hazard to navigation, the government has scuttled a derelict freighter on the north side to provide a visual marker and a radar reflector as well.

A pair of Red Sea bannerfish move down the sloping wall of Gordon Reef. (Photo: Esther Ratterree)

The dive will usually begin at the southwest corner of the reef in a mild current running west to east. The dive along the south side is a sloping wall of sand and coral boulders to about 65 feet (20 meters), where the sheer wall begins and drops to 225 feet (70 meters). At the east end of the reef, the current picks up to provide a wild (up to 2 knots) ride around the tip to the north side along a sheer wall that extends from the surface to the depths below. This sheer wall is covered with many soft corals and fan corals. Throughout the dive, you should be on the lookout for pelagic animals in the blue water. Continue riding the current that will subside once you turn the northeast corner, and you will find yourself in a sandy flat area 40 feet (12 meters) deep, with small coral heads and many reef fish.

Two bluecheek butterflyfish emerge from an overhang along a wall.

◀ At the east end of Gordon Reef, the current picks up speed and propels you past a wall covered with various colored soft corals.

Jackson Reef 10

Location:	In the Straights of Tiran
Attractions:	Sloping wall, strong currents, and large pelagic fish
Typical depth range:	10–225 feet (3–70 meters)
Access:	Drift dive, boat dive, local guide
Expertise required:	Novice with instructor, advanced to dive master/instructor

Jackson is the northernmost of a string of reefs that begins at Gordon to the southwest, and is followed by Thomas, Wood House, and finally Jackson. The diving procedure is similar to Gordon, where you begin on the south side of the reef. You will find a sloping dropoff with a plateau at 30 to 60 feet (10 to 20 meters), then the dropoff continues to 225 feet (70 meters).

Strong currents will provide you with a good ride around the northeast end of the reef to a shallow sandy bay on the north side. Here there are large numbers of schooling reef fish, including colorful schools of yellow goatfish. There are always encounters with large pelagic animals along the drift dive on the south side if you are alert to the surroundings.

It seems that on every dive, you will encounter a large humphead wrasse, and Jackson Reef is no exception. This one has a few ramoras hanging on for a free ride. (Photo: Esther Ratterree) ►

A goatfish pauses in the light current along Jackson Reef before continuing its search for food with its feelers in the sandy bottom.

Coral Garden (Hushasha) 11

Location: Southwest coastline of Tiran Island
Attractions: Small sloping wall to sandy bottom with many coral heads and shallow caves
Typical depth range: 10–75 feet (3–23 meters)
Access: Boat dive, local guide
Expertise required: Novice to advanced

Coral Gardens, also called Hushasha, is a sandy shelf that extends from the shore of Tiran Island at a gradual slope to a depth of 75 feet (23 meters). Throughout this sandy shelf are many large and small coral heads that are abundant with marine life. They also provide many crevices and shallow caves to explore where you will find colorful butterfly fish, Red Sea bannerfish, regal and emperor angelfish. There are also many lionfish in the caves and crevices, and bluespotted stingrays can be found on the sand under small overhangs.

The boat will use a mooring and the dive will finish and end at the moored boat. This is an excellent site for still and macro photography and videography because the still waters allow for settling in the sand for those hard to get closeups that are impossible to obtain on a drift dive.

Coral polyps are out feeding on this animal, and their opening and closing movements are very quick and interesting to watch. ►

A slashed butterflyfish stands out against the blue background of a wall at Coral Gardens.

Koshkasha 12

Location:	South side of Tiran Island
Attractions:	Small bay with sandy bottom, many large coral heads and shallow caves
Typical depth range:	20–50 feet (3–23 meters)
Access:	Boat dive, local guide
Expertise required:	Novice to advanced

This site is a bay located on the south side of Tiran Island. It is used for a night anchorage by liveaboard dive boats that operate in the area. The bottom is about 50 feet (23 meters) deep and has many large coral heads and shallow caves covered with marine life. Because it is a good night anchorage, it is also a good night-dive location. The coral heads come alive at night with many colored feather stars. The large areas of antler coral house many reef fish for their nightly accommodations. The bottom seems to have bluespotted stingrays everywhere, and some crevices house an octopus or two.

The sandy bottom at the base of coral heads is frequented by the bluespotted stingray like this one, and are sometimes completely covered with sand.

The colorful longjaw squirrelfish moves about an overhang at the Koshkasha dive site on the south side of Tiran Island.

A crocodile fish eyes a feather worm as if waiting to pounce on it.

Abu Tinun 13

Location: Reef, off the eastern end of Tiran Island
Attractions: Sandy shelf with sea-grasses
Typical depth range: 20–50 feet (3–23 meters)
Access: Boat dive, local guide
Expertise required: Novice to advanced

Located between Tiran Island and Sinafar Island, Abu Tinun consists of a sandy shelf, sea grasses, and coral heads. The sea grasses are home to cuttlefish, stingrays, eels, and many seahorses. The coral heads have many cleaning stations where you will find large groupers, sweetlips, and jacks awaiting their turns for the cleaner wrasses to remove pesky parasites. There are also some caves and overhangs on these coral heads, and some contain black coral trees. Longnose hawkfish are found on these coral trees, and when lit with a strong light, they are bright red in color.

Most butterflyfish pair up for life, and always stay together. These bluecheek butterflyfish are no exception.

Sinafar Island 14

Location:	Eastern end of the Straights of Tiran
Attractions:	Sheer wall to a sloping shelf with canyons and caves
Typical depth range:	20–120 feet (3–37 meters)
Access:	Boat dive, local guide
Expertise required:	Novice with instructor, advanced, dive master/instructor

The southeast end of Sinafar Island is an incredible dive site. It starts with a wall at the surface that stretches to a depth of 30 feet (10 meters) then slopes to a coral reef with sandy canyons extending to the bottom depths. Some of these canyons have sheer sides covered from the surface to the bottom with various colored soft corals. There are many caves, with one starting at 60 feet (18 meters) at a small fan coral framed opening. It then extends in 50 feet (15 meters) and gets larger all of the time until it becomes a chamber 10 feet (3 meters) high by 20 feet (6 meters) wide. The chamber

An isolated lyretail coralfish is probably looking around for company because coral fish are usually found in large schools that cover the reef in a blanket of red.

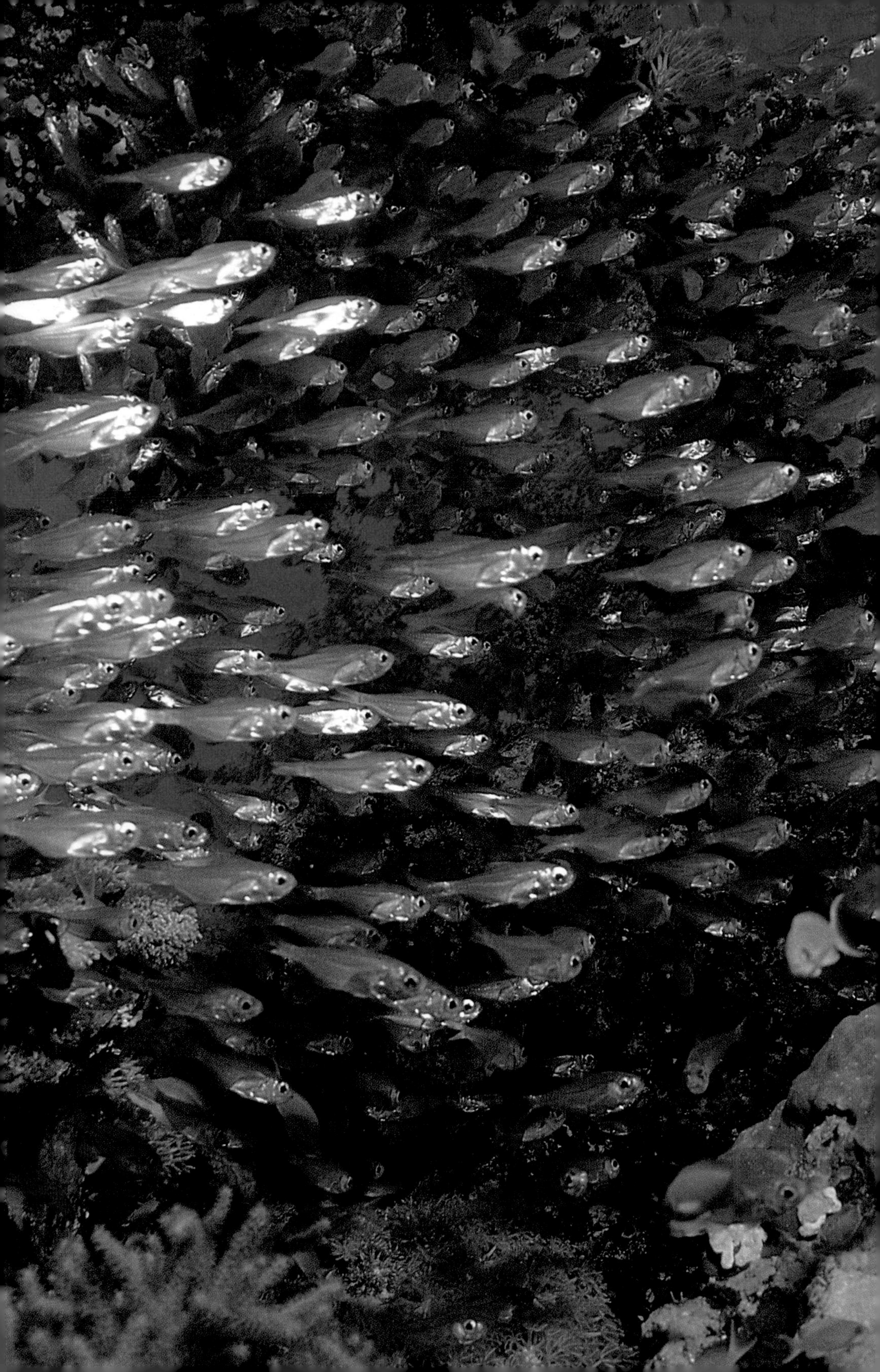

A diver views some coral heads while the wall looms behind at Sinafar Island.

◄ Glass sweeper fish are photographed in a magnificent cave at Sinafar Island's eastern end.

has a small chimney in the top and a large window to the blue water at 50 feet (15 meters) on the side of a wall. While swimming through the cave, you are constantly surrounded by sweeper glass fish that slowly move aside to let you through. In the chamber, the concentration of these fish can obliterate the large opening to the reef, and as they slowly move aside, the blue water of the opening appears as if a curtain is being drawn back.

On the sandy slope are amphoras from an ancient wreck believed to be from the Ottoman Empire. This area has large table corals, and the amphoras are found in between these corals. These amphoras were filled with mercury, and some may still have some remnants of this cargo if you look closely.

Flasher Reef 15

Location: Between Sinafar Island and Shusha Island to the east
Attractions: Flashlight Fish!!!!
Typical depth range: 20–60 feet (3–18 meters)
Access: Boat dive, local guide
Expertise required: Novice with instructor, advanced, dive master/instructor

As you may have guessed, the best time to dive here is at night. The flashlight fish are everywhere, and you only have to turn off your light and they will surround you. The area surrounding the reef is a sandy bottom with a lot of sea grasses, and wonderful hermit crabs, seahorses, and stingrays. The reef itself is frequented by turtles, rays, and the most impressive Spanish dancer nudibrachs. It is a real treat to watch a Spanish dancer dance in the beam of your dive light for more than ten minutes. It is even better to have it dance in your video lights with the camcorder running. If your dive boat

A bluespotted stingray glides across the sandy bottom on a night dive at Flasher Reef.

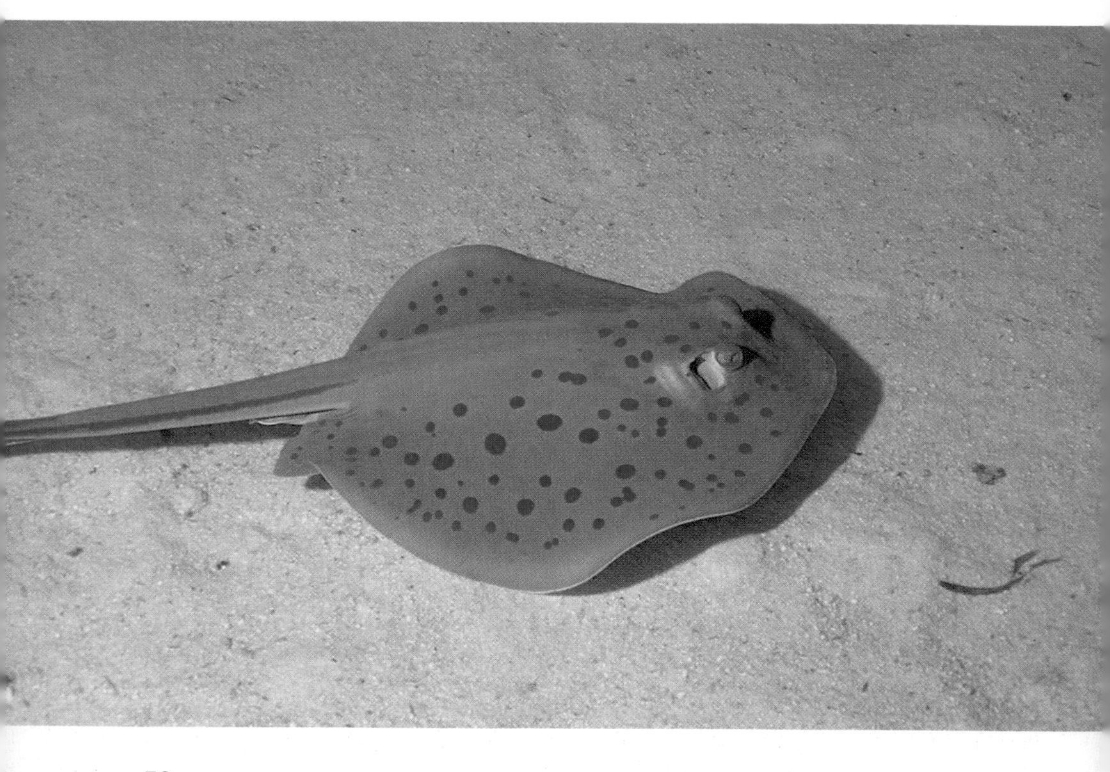

Brittlestars are decorated with fire coral branches on this coral head on Flasher Reef.

has lights that shine in the water, you will find yourself in a school of squid as you return to the boat. They will rapidly change color for you as they move in and out of your dive light.

A turtle leisurely swims by in the deep blue water.

Tower 16

Location: North of Sharm El Sheikh Harbor
Attractions: Steep wall with caves
Typical depth range: 10–195 feet (3–60 meters)
Access: Drift boat dive, local guide
Expertise required: Novice with instructor, advanced, dive master/instructor

Located between Na'ama Bay and Sharm El Sheikh Harbor, this site is very popular and has earned a reputation as an exciting dive. The wall drops from a shallow reef table immediately offshore to a depth of 195 feet (60 meters). The drift dive will start up-current, and as you descend along the wall you will encounter fan corals much larger than a diver. This is an excellent opportunity to frame a diver with one of these fans, taking extreme care not to come in contact with the fan and damage it. The current is usually mild, which makes this a great drift dive for photographers.

Some of the caves along the wall actually go up and exit to the shallow reef table above. In these caves you will find schools of glass sweepers, soft corals, and pairs of Red Sea bannerfish ready to pose for the perfect picture. While swimming or drifting along the wall, you will encounter many jacks, and an occasional pelagic animal as well. Also found in the overhangs are wonderful large soft corals of every color imaginable, and if you look very closely you may see a longnose hawkfish perched on these soft coral stalks.

Soft corals hang down from the tops of overhangs along the steep wall of the Tower dive site. ►

◄ As you drift along the wall at the Tower, you will encounter pelagic fish swimming up-current coming to meet you.

Ras Um Sid 17

Location: North Point of Sharm El Sheikh Harbor
Attractions: Moderate slope with large coral heads
Typical depth range: 20–80 feet (6–25 meters)
Access: Shore dive, boat dive, local guide
Expertise required: Snorkeler, novice, advanced, dive master/instructor

From a coral shelf that starts at the shore, the reef slopes gradually to a depth of 80 feet (25 meters) to a sandy bottom. On the sloped wall, you can find coral heads with large fan corals. These coral heads are home to many reef fish, including the magnificent lionfish. Off the reef in the blue water are many pelagic animals, and you can see barracudas, rays, and sharks on many dives at this site. Usually the dive boat will attach to the provided mooring and diving will start and end at the mooring line.

While passing an overhang at Ras Um Sid, this bigeye changed from silver to bright red in a matter of seconds. ▶

It is an unusual event to find a stonefish off a camouflaged background such as this one at Ras Um Sid dive site.

Temple 18

Location:	North side of Sharm El Sheikh Harbor
Attractions:	Pinnacles
Typical depth range:	10–65 feet (3–20 meters)
Access:	Boat dive, local guide
Expertise required:	Snorkeler, novice, advanced, dive master/ instructor

The Temple is a group of three pinnacles that rise up from the sandy bottom at 65 feet (20 meters) to the surface. These pinnacles are in close proximity to each other, with sand channels between them. The sheer walls of the pinnacles have many fan corals, soft corals, hard corals, and reef fish that cover them in a blanket of color. There are plenty of lionfish gliding about, while stonefish stay motionless, camouflaged and invisible on the coral heads. Schools of glass sweepers move in unison around and between the pinnacles, as if performing a ballet.

Because of its close proximity to Sharm El Sheikh and Na'ama Bay and because it is a safe night mooring, the Temple is a popular night-dive loca-

Ras Muhammed National Park

Ras Muhammed National Park lies within the boundaries of the Sinai National Park and has some special regulations and requirements. You must have a full visitors visa in your passport to dive in this park. The mini visa you can get at the airport upon arrival in Egypt will not allow you to dive here. Your passport will be held by the dive operator or the park officer any time you are within the park boundaries. A fee of U.S. $10 per person is charged for each diving day. This fee will be collected and a receipt given to you by the dive shop or liveaboard boat operator.

The park regulations are posted at the park office, and a pamphlet detailing the park rules should be given to you with the receipt from the dive shop or liveaboard dive operators. The following are the main regulations to keep in mind at all times in the park:

- Stay on marked roads. There are numerous hazards covered by sands in the desert.
- Dive in designated diving areas only. Do not walk or anchor on the reef.
- Fishing and spearfishing are prohibited as is the removal or damage of any material, living or dead (such as coral, shells, fish, plants, fossils, etc.) from the park.
- Camping is allowed only in designated areas of the park. Otherwise, all visitors must leave this park at sunset.

tion for day and liveaboard boats. The Temple becomes magical at night. The pinnacles are covered with soft corals and feather stars in many colors, and the basket stars create laced curtain plumes in the light current as they feed. As you approach the basket stars with your dive light, they will tend to withdraw into a ball. By moving your light away, they again expand to their laced net position and continue feeding. Shine your dive light back in crevices and find sleeping parrotfish, some with their cocoons around them.

◀ The Temple dive site comes alive at night with vibrant colors, as this soft coral animal shows off well. (Photo: Esther Ratterree)

By looking back in the crevices at the Temple with your dive light on night dives you will see Parrotfish sleeping.

A view of Ras Muhammed from the sea. Ras is Arabic for head. Thus this is the head of Muhammed. By looking at the point where the land meets the water, you can almost see a head. (Photo: Esther Ratterree)

Ras Za'atir 19

Location:	North tip of the Ras Muhammed Peninsula (within the boundaries of Ras Muhammed National Park)
Attractions:	Steep wall, many pelagic animals, and large caves
Typical depth range:	20–165 feet (6–50 meters)
Access:	Drift boat dive, local guide
Expertise required:	Novice with instructor, advanced, dive master/ instructor

The current generally runs from the north point to the south into a cove along this sheer wall. There are some large caves near the point that are filled with glass sweepers and soft corals. Deeper along the wall, trees of black coral with their resident longnose hawkfishes abound. The shallow areas of the wall are excellent for macro photography, because they contain many small invertebrates, such as nudibranchs, corals, and feather tube worms. Large pelagic animals frequent this wall and because it is less dived than nearby Ras Muhammed (Shark Reef), some shy sharks, barracudas, and manta rays can be seen here as often, if not more so, than at its famous neighbor.

There are many overhangs on the wall at Ras Za'atir with colorful soft corals hanging from them.

Fisherman's Bank 20

Location: North side of the Ras Muhammed Peninsula (within the boundaries of Ras Muhammed National Park)
Attractions: Shallow coral reef, colorful fish
Typical depth range: 10–80 feet (3–25 meters)
Access: Shore dive, boat dive, local guide
Expertise required: Snorkeler, novice to advanced

Fisherman's Bank is a popular shore dive from within Ras Muhammed National Park. The reef is located offshore a short distance from the beach for easy access. The top of the reef is sand with a sloping dropoff. You will find many colorful reef fishes here. These include the yellowband (Map) angelfish, emperor angelfish, regal angelfish, and many pairs of bluecheek butterflyfish. There are some small caves and a few stingrays to be found on the bottom.

Snorkelers enjoy a beautiful day at Fisherman's Bank in the Ras Muhammed National Park.

Ras Muhammed (Shark Reef) 21

Location:	Tip of the Ras Muhammed Peninsula (within the boundaries of the Ras Muhammed National Park)
Attractions:	Vertical wall, Anemone City, and Shark Reef
Typical depth range:	30–300 feet (10–90 meters)
Access:	Drift dive, boat dive, local guide
Expertise required:	Snorkeler, novice with instructor, advanced, dive master/instructor

More has been written about Ras Muhammed than any other single dive site in the world, and all of it is good. There is a profound reason for all of this praise. No other single dive site comes to mind that offers so many different wonderful diving conditions in such a small area. There is beach access for snorkelers and shore divers, and of course, mooring sites for boat divers. Ras Muhammed starts at the point of the peninsula with an incredible wall descending from the surface to depths of over 300 feet (90 meters). When diving along this wall, you can see sharks, jacks, and other large pelagic ani-

This humphead wrasse in the channel at Ras Muhammed is accustomed to photographers and will probably soon have an agent to negotiate contacts for it.

mals as they pass here from the Red Sea on their way into and out of the Gulf of Aqaba.

As you travel south along the wall, you enter a bay where the wall starts to slope to a series of sandy shelves below. At 60 feet (18 meters), the bay starts to turn back toward the sea, and here you will encounter Anemone City. This is a shelf on the reef covered with many anemones that are bustling with their resident clown anemonefish. Clown anemonefish are in such profusion it is hard to get past here with any film left in your camera.

The reef continues out toward the sea where it meets two submerged islands perched on a sandy slope that descends into the abyss of the Red Sea. These submerged islands are called Shark Reef. Between these islands and the shore are the moorings for dive boats. Usually you will begin your dive up-current around the Ras Muhammed wall and drift with the currents past Anemone City to the north tip of Shark Reef. Then depending on the currents, you will proceed in circling Shark Reef in either a clockwise or

A profusion of color and motion abounds at Anemone City, Ras Muhammed where colonies of anemones and their resident clown anemonefish cover the reef area. (Photo: Robert Stribling)

◄ In the sandy channel between Shark Reef and the shore at Ras Muhammed, a map angelfish is brilliant against the sun-filtered waters.

This large moray eel is on a stage with red soft coral side lights. This eel is a resident of the mooring area at Ras Muhammed.

◀ If you look very hard in the channel at Ras Muhammed you will find some of these crocodile fish in the sand. They will stay motionless unless you get too close or move toward them too quickly. (Photo: Esther Ratterree)

counterclockwise direction. On the outside of these reefs you will experience a magnificent dropoff covered with large fan corals, soft corals, and resident fishes in great profusion. Off the wall you will see many large pelagic animals, including sharks, rays, and large groups of schooling jacks.

As you complete your circumnavigation of Shark Reef, you will ascend to the sandy channel between Shark Reef and the shore. Here you will find the remnants of a freighter sunk in the late 60s with a cargo of pipe and bathroom fixtures. Although the wreck itself slid down the sandy slope to unknown depths in 1986, some fixtures and other items of its cargo still remain for you to see. Some of the reef animals have taken up residence in these remnants, and it can be quite amusing to see a moray eel come out of a toilet fixture. This sandy area is also frequented by very large trumpetfish in groups, and they make an interesting contrast with their straight lines against the sandy bottom.

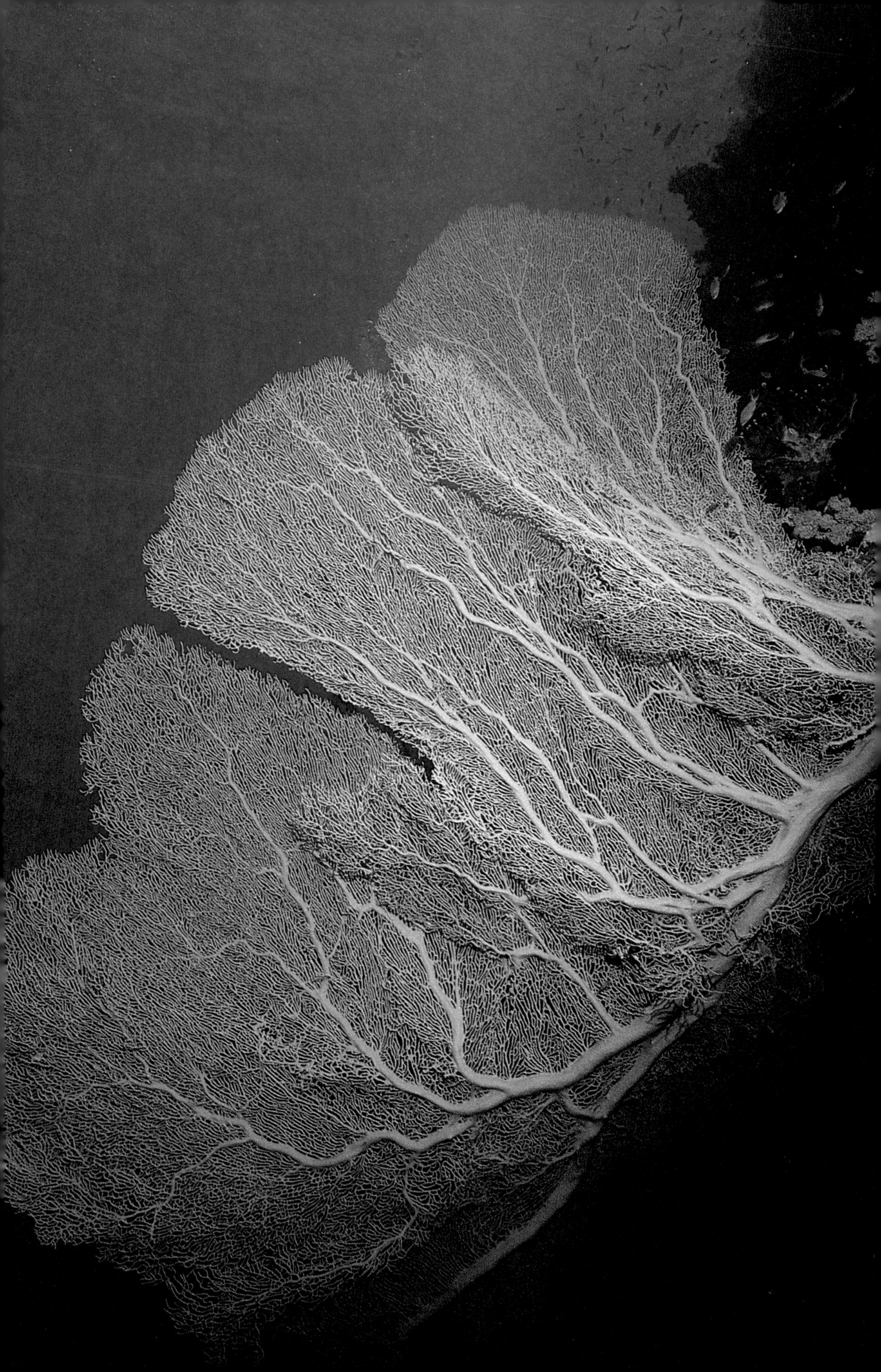

Alternatives 22

Location:	East side of the Ras Muhammed Peninsula in the Gulf of Suez (within the boundaries of Ras Muhammed National Park)
Attractions:	Coral heads, small walls, and colorful fish
Typical depth range:	20–60 feet (6–18 meters)
Access:	Boat dive, local guide
Expertise required:	Novice to advanced

The Alternatives are located in the Gulf of Suez, which is sometimes subject to unpredictable winds and storms. As such, dive boat operators need a safe mooring to sit out these usually short periods of inclement weather and to serve as an acceptable dive site at the same time. The Alternatives fill this need well, and this is how they derived their name.

The Alternatives area is a fringing reef with a large lagoon in the center with a group of loosely connected submerged islands forming the ring. The boat will usually moor in the lagoon, and divers will swim out as if along spokes of a wheel from the center hub. The best diving is on the outside walls of the ring islands, with small walls and many large coral heads offering all varieties of marine life and fishes. Because this is a safe mooring, night dives here are very common. On these night dives, good planning should be used to make sure that on your swim out from the boat, you swim to one of the ring islands and not out one of the channels between them into the open sea.

◀ *Along the outside wall of Shark Reef, Ras Muhammed, you will find large fan corals that are sometimes larger than a diver.*

When backlighted this coral animal takes on the appearance of an alien visitor.

Beacon Rock (*Dunraven Wreck*) 23

Location:	South side of the Ras Muhammed Peninsula (within the boundaries of Ras Muhammed National Park)
Attractions:	*Dunraven Wreck*
Typical depth range:	90–130 feet (27–40 meters)
Access:	Boat dive, local guide
Expertise required:	Advanced to dive master/instructor

The *Dunraven* was a turn-of-the-century steam freighter, and it is rumored to have been a spy ship for T. E. Lawrence (Lawrence of Arabia). The ship hit the reef, or was sunk off Beacon Rock, a jetty off of the Ras Muhammed Peninsula in the Gulf of Suez.

The wreck lies on its side and is badly deteriorated. The boiler room and its boiler, however, are very much in tack and accessible from a hole in the side. This area is overgrown with soft corals and filled with glass sweepers that move about in orderly procession. In the damaged stern area, you may see some lionfish gliding lazily along amongst these glass sweepers, and with a sudden burst, they may gobble up some of these small fish for lunch.

The boat will moor at Beacon Rock, and you will swim down the face of the wall to the wreck and return the same way. If there is a strong current at the site, the dive will probably be omitted or aborted if underway. The depth and location of this wreck make it a dive for advanced or dive master/instructors only.

Sha'ab Ali (*Thistlegorm Wreck*) 24

Location: North side of the Straights of Gubal, in the Gulf of Suez
Attractions: *Thistlegorm Wreck*
Typical depth range: 60–120 feet (18–37 meters)
Access: Boat dive, local guide
Expertise required: Advanced to dive master/instructor

The *Thistlegorm Wreck* first gained notoriety in Jacques Cousteau's 1950s book on the Red Sea. Its location since that time remained a mystery until 1992 when it was rediscovered by a group of sport divers.

The *Thistlegorm* was a British munitions ship bringing supplies to the British units fighting Rommel's forces in the African Desert. It was sunk by German bombs before it had a chance to deliver its cargo, and although

Soft corals and reef fish have congregated in a tender car on the deck of the Thistlegorm Wreck, *and give the appearance of a planted floral arrangement.*

◀ *An emperor angelfish moves across the hull of the* Dunraven Wreck *at the Beacon Rock dive site.*

the rear portion of the ship was blown away, there is still a lot of interesting items to see.

On the forward deck are rail cars, including a tender car that has become a planter box for both hard and soft corals. The addition of some colorful fish make it look like a planned floral display. Also, in the rear hold are many rubber boots still in good condition after all these years of submersion. Another attraction is the locomotive engine resting upright in the sand at 120 feet (37 meters) off the port side of the ship. The eerie feeling you experience looking head on into a large engine through the reduced visibility of the water can be quite memorable.

The visibility at this site can vary from great to nothing in a short amount of time. This fact, coupled with the depth of the wreck, make it advisable for only advanced divers or dive master/instructors. The dive boat will moor to the wreck, and you will have to work with the currents to and from this mooring.

A bluespotted stingray is stunned by the camera flash while moving along the sand at night.

Gubal Island 25

Location: South side of the Straights of Gubal
Attractions: Protected cove and spectacular wall
Typical depth range: 10–120 feet (2–37 meters)
Access: Boat dive, local guide
Expertise required: Novice with instructor, advanced, dive master/instructor

Gubal is an island located on the south side of the Straights of Gubal. It is one island of an archipelago that stretches from the Egyptian mainland south to Hurghada. On the south side of the island is a protected bay that offers safe mooring and the added benefit of being an exciting dive site.

Night diving here is excellent, especially in the mooring area. You can dive under the boat and explore the tidal shelf that slopes gradually down to the bottom of the bay. This shelf is loaded with marine invertebrates and reef fishes. There are also many large mollusks such as the Triton's trum-

A large Triton's trumpet glides across the sand at Gubal Island on a night dive. The mollusk is in search of its favorite food the crown of thorns starfish.

If you use your imagination, this urchin appears to be lighted from the inside, and resembles a glowing flying saucer.

pet that come out at night and display their mantels as they move along the reef in search of the crown-of-thorns starfish, their favorite meal.

In the daytime, the wall that extends from the bay into the Straights is spectacular. There are many pelagic animals and a lot of dolphins that swim close to get a good view of the divers in the water. This is a drift dive that starts from the bay with the current taking you out toward the Straights. Care must be taken to make sure you don't get carried away from the group and dive boat.

Abu Nuhas (Ships' Graveyard) 26

Location:	South entrance to the Straights of Gubal
Attractions:	Multiple shipwrecks
Typical depth range:	30–85 feet (10–25 meters)
Access:	Boat dive, local guide
Expertise required:	Advanced to dive master/instructor

Abu Nuhas is a group of small submerged islands that have over the years lured unsuspecting ships aground. The ships then sunk along the sloping walls of these reefs. The area is unprotected and subject to weather extremes, so diving here is a treat. The boat will usually moor to the wreck of a barge on the northeast point that has a moderate slope from the surface to the sandy bottom. Although this wreck is not all that exciting, a short swim along the sloping wall will yield the reward of a large freighter. This wreck is on its side at a depth of 85 feet (25 meters) and is relatively free of hazardous debris, making it an enjoyable dive.

Schools of glass sweeper fish are in the bridge and hold areas, and resident emperor angelfish on the deck stick to their territories and do not swim away from divers as they tend to do on the reef. There are also some large resident moray eels to be visited while in the wreck, and they will be sure to excite you if you happen upon one in a dark hold with the beam of your light finding it first.

A diver hovers above a wreck on Abu Nuhas Reef in the Gulf of Suez. (Photo: Esther Ratterree)

El-Akhawein (The Brothers) 27

Location:	In the Red Sea off the Egyptian coast, south of Safaga
Attractions:	Sheer dropoff along walls and pelagic animals
Typical depth range:	20–300 feet (6–90 meters)
Access:	Boat dive, local guide
Expertise required:	Dive master/instructor

El-Akhawein, or The Brothers as they are commonly known, are situated in the Red Sea south of the Sinai Peninsula off the coast of the Egyptian mainland south of Safaga. Their steep vertical dropoffs rival those of Ras Muhammed, and because there are fewer divers, the fish are unafraid and bolder. Here you can see mantas, eagle rays, barracuda, and sharks including the impressive hammerheads.

With its remoteness, which is beneficial to the profuse animal life, comes a major drawback. There is no where to hide when storms come up on the sea and there are no emergency services on these islands, including search and rescue in case of emergency. Added to this problem are the depth and currents that you will encounter on a given dive, including some that will take you down and shoot you back up in a matter of seconds.

Because of these problems, at the present time this site should be for only experienced dive masters and instructors. With the number of divers coming to this area, it is only a matter of time before emergency and other services are provided to these islands and other remote dive sites in the Red Sea.

Soft coral has taken up a home on this large fan coral on the wall at The Brothers Islands in the Red Sea. (Photo: Esther Ratterree) ▶

A school of yellow goatfish congregate in the shallows out of the currents of a reef.

Sha'ab Su'adi (Toyota Wreck) 28

Location:	In the Red Sea off the Sudan coast, north of Port Sudan
Attractions:	Sloping reef with wreck of sunken freighter, loaded with Toyota cars
Typical depth range:	10–220 feet (3–70 meters)
Access:	Boat dive, local guide
Expertise required:	Dive master/instructor

As with all dive sites in this part of the Red Sea, this area can only be accessed safely during very good weather conditions. As there is no land mass for protection, any high winds or waves can be extremely dangerous for mooring and diving activities; thus, the dive master/instructor expertise level is assigned to this site.

The reef at Sha'ab Su'adi has beautiful coral gardens with the main attraction being that of the Toyota Wreck. This freighter (*Blue Bell*) was sunk in 1979 and is loaded with Toyota cars. For this reason, the site is commonly called the Toyota Wreck. At a depth of 25 feet (7 meters), you find a marvelous truck covered with soft corals and other parts of the wreckage. Here you can see the bow of the sunken freighter which extends to a depth of 225 feet (70 meters) and houses the resident giant grouper.

At the dropoff you can find manta rays and Napoleon wrasses that swim by from time to time. There are also nice coral gardens around the wreck in shallower water that offer good colorful photographic and videographic opportunities of colorful fish and marine life.

◀ A diver relaxes on a drift dive along a wall in the Red Sea.

Nudibrach makes its residence and moves about freely on one of the cars on the Toyota Wreck. ▶

Sha'ab Roumi 29

Location:	In the Red Sea off the Sudan coast, north of Port Sudan
Attractions:	Atoll with fantastic corals and remains of Cousteau's *Precontinent II & III*
Typical depth range:	10–100 feet (3–30 meters)
Access:	Boat dive, local guide
Expertise required:	Dive master/instructor

Northeast of Port Sudan is Sha'ab Roumi, an atoll that was made famous through Cousteau's experiment, *Precontinent II & III.* On this fantastic atoll the participants lived and dived for half a year. They left behind a small underwater city that now houses a great deal of marine life instead of divers. At a depth of 26 to 33 feet (8 to 10 meters) is a garage for a submarine that is now covered with colorful corals, sponges, and other marine animals, and on the side is a little yard with beautiful soft corals. Continuing down the reef to 100 feet (30 meters) in the blue water on the dropoff, you can see a shark cage, which is nearly overgrown and has become part of the reef structure.

Diving around this atoll, you will find many schools of fish. The beauty of this atoll with its giant corals presents a stark contrast to the land that surrounds it. Even with the difficulties of weather, dependable diving/liveaboard operations, and local political strife, a visit to this atoll will allow you to find all the best that the Red Sea offers. During good weather, you can anchor in the lagoon and, if you are lucky, you can see dolphins that appear to be sleeping there.

◀ *Vibrant soft corals grow on and around the Toyota Wreck at Sha'ab Su'adi, Sudan diving site. (Photo: Esther Ratterree)*

Sponge incrusted fan coral is found on the wall at Sha'ab Roumi, Sudan. ▶

Sanganeb 30

Location: In the Red Sea off the Sudan coast, north of Port Sudan
Attractions: Underwater plateau with soft corals and schools of pelagic fish
Typical depth range: 20–115 feet (6–35 meters)
Access: Boat dive, local guide
Expertise required: Dive master/instructor

Sanganeb is a reef with its own lighthouse and concrete observation platform. From this platform Professor Eibl-Eibesfeld composed his acclaimed book *Thousand Atolls.* While diving here, the famous diver and underwater photographer Hans Hass reported his first meeting with a great white shark, thus, this area has had an attraction for marine scientists and explorers for some time.

On the south tip is a large underwater plateau at nearly 100 feet (30 meters) covered with some of the most beautiful soft corals to be encountered in the Red Sea. The plateau abounds with schools of barracudas, eagle rays, many little sharks, and interesting caves. You will also see small schools of hammerheads and a few manta rays swimming by in a leisurely manner.

If weather conditions permit, (no north winds) you may be able to dive on the north point of the atoll. There is a dream of underwater scenery, which begins at a depth of 33 feet (10 meters) and descends to 100 feet (30 meters). You will be engulfed in light pink colored soft corals and discover a paradise for wide-angle photographers/videographers! You will find hundreds of barracudas, big sharks, even Makos and schools of hammerheads.

◀ Fiery colors are found all over the Sha'ab Roumi Atoll area. (Photo: Esther Ratterree)

A silvery jack comes up from the depths along the wall at Sanganeb Atoll. ▶

Wingate Reef (*Umbria Wreck*) 31

Location:	In the Red Sea off the Sudan coast, east of Port Sudan
Attractions:	Wreck of the *Umbria*
Typical depth range:	50–130 feet (15–40 meters)
Access:	Boat dive, local guide
Expertise required:	Dive master/instructor

Wingate Reef is about an hour sailing time from Port Sudan, and is the ultimate dream of every European diver. Forty-five years ago the crew of the *Umbria* scuttled their own ship at the start of World War II. You will find a colorful grown up wreck with many tamed fish you can watch from a short distance. Sometimes you will see large groupers that are taking care of the wartime cargo of the ship. The wreck is a photographers/videographers dream in which a diver can easily swim down the ship's gangways and photograph diving companions with the giant scenery of the wreck in the background and the sunlight reflecting from the surface.

◀ *A diver examines the underwater plateau that extends out from the dropoff at Sanganeb Atoll, Sudan.*

A diver explores the Umbria Wreck *at Wingate Reef, Sudan.*

Dahlak Islands (Eritrea) 32

Location:	In the Red Sea off the Eritrea coast
Attractions:	Sheer dropoffs along walls and pelagic animals
Typical depth range:	30–230 feet (6–70 meters)
Access:	Boat dive, local guide
Expertise required:	Dive master/instructor

This is an archipelago made up of many islands that rise up from the sandy bottom of the Red Sea to become islands ranging from small rocky outcroppings to large islands with long sandy beaches. At present this area is accessible only by long range liveaboard dive operators and is subject to extreme weather and political limitations.

The diving on these islands is made up of colorful reefs with sheer dropoffs that extend to the sandy bottom at 230 feet (70 meters). These walls are covered with many soft and fan corals, and there are numerous schools of pelagic fish, including sharks, barracuda, jacks, and even manta rays to be viewed as they swim by on their way to and from the narrow straights that separate the Red Sea from the Gulf of Aden and the Arabian Sea.

◀ *Hundreds of coral polyps feed frantically on plankton drifting by on the* Umbria *wreck. (Photo: Esther Ratterree)*

Colorful soft corals blend with the blue background and the reef to paint a vivid picture that will last in the minds of divers long after a visit to the Red Sea. ▶

4

Safety

Emergency Services in Sharm El Sheikh

Sharm El Sheikh now has a DAN certified recompression chamber that exceeds many U. S. Navy standards and is run by personnel who have been trained thoroughly in its proper use and maintenance. The contact for this recompression chamber in Sharm is telephone numbers (062) 600922 or 600923, and their FAX number is (062) 601011.

Dangerous Marine Animals

There is minimal danger from marine animals in the Red Sea, and with just a little common sense and presence of mind, even this danger can be eliminated.

Sharks. Because the feeding of fish and spearfishing is prohibited in all diving areas of the Red Sea, there is very little danger from these animals.

Eels. These animals normally try to avoid divers. They will back into their holes if approached or harassed. The BITE! is the most common injury from these animals and is a direct result of divers feeding them either by accident or by the diver holding onto the food for too long or too close.

Lionfish. The dorsal spines on these animals are highly venomous and, depending on your body's reaction, can be serious. If harassed, lionfish can move with incredible speed and deliver a painful sting. However, most injuries result from a diver resting on or inadvertently bumping into these animals.

Scorpionfish, stonefish. These animals camouflage themselves so well that they are almost impossible to see when they are not moving. Like the lionfish, they have venomous dorsal fins that can deliver a painful to serious sting if you come into contact with them. They do not however attack, so with good buoyancy control and reef protection in mind you should not have to experience this pain.

Scorpionfish and stonefish are very hard to see. You must always be aware they can be present in unusual places as is this one.

Stingrays. They don't call them stingrays for nothing. These animals have a sharp barbed stinger on the top of their tail where it meets their body. This stinger is venomous, and the barbs cause more tissue damage when pulled out than when they enter. *Do not* grab one of these animals or settle on one while kneeling on the bottom to take photos.

Crown of thorns starfish. The tips of the thorns contain a very powerful venom, and the thorns tend to break off leaving a small piece of the thorn to become infected. Many complications can occur from a crown of thorns wound, so it is best to see a doctor immediately.

Barracuda. These sleek animals with the big teeth are curious, but not a danger to divers. They tend to attack loose and quickly moving shiny objects (like small bait fish), so don't wear a tin foil wet suit.

Preparation

Before you leave on your trip be sure all your diving equipment has been serviced and is functioning properly. You should always test all existing or any newly purchased equipment in a pool or the ocean to ensure it is working and to familiarize yourself with something new. This is true for any photographic or video equipment also, but it is more important for your life-support diving equipment. Make sure you have a valid certification card with you and a log book that is up-to-date. Install new batteries in your dive computer, and refresh yourself on its proper safe operation. Some resorts and boat operations require a proficiency check, so if you haven't dived for some time arrange for a refresher course at your local dive shop prior to your departure.

Diver Guidelines for Protecting Fragile Marine Habitats

1. Maintain proper buoyancy control and avoid over-weighting.
2. Use correct weight belt position to stay horizontal, i.e., raise the belt above your waist to elevate your feet/fins, and move it lower toward your hips to lower them.
3. Use your tank position in the backpack as a balance weight, i.e., raise your backpack on the tank to lower your legs, and lower the backpack on the tank to raise your legs.
4. Watch for buoyancy changes during a dive trip. During the first couple of days, you'll probably breathe a little harder and need a bit more weight than the last few days.
5. Be careful about buoyancy loss at depth; the deeper you go the more your wet suit compresses, and the more buoyancy you lose.
6. Photographers must be extra careful. Cameras and equipment affect buoyancy. Changing f-stops, framing a subject, and maintaining position for a photo often conspire to prohibit the ideal "no-touch" approach on a reef. So, when you must use "holdfasts," choose them intelligently.
7. Avoid full leg kicks when working close to the bottom and when leaving a photo scene. When you inadvertently kick something, stop kicking! Seems obvious, but some divers either semi-panic or are totally oblivious when they bump something.
8. When swimming in strong currents, be extra careful about leg kicks and handholds.
9. Attach dangling gauges, computer consoles, and octopus regulators. They are like miniature wrecking balls to a reef.
10. Never drop boat anchors onto a reef.

* Condensed from "Diver Guidelines" by Chris Newbert© Oceanica 1991. Reprinted with permission of Oceanica and Chris Newbert. If you are interested in more information or in helping Oceanica preserve our ocean realm, please write to Oceanica, 342 West Sunset, San Antonio, Texas 78209, USA.

Appendix

Dive Operators

The list below is included as a service to the reader. The list is as accurate as possible at the time of printing. This list does not constitute an endorsement of these facilities. If operators/owners wish to be included in future reprints/editions, please contact Pisces Books, P.O. Box 2608, Houston, Texas 77252-2608.

Aqaba, Jordan

Hotel-Club Aquamarina, Aqaba
P.O. Box 96
Aqaba, Jordan
03-316250/1/2/3/4

Eilat, Israel

Aqua Sport International
Coral Beach
P.O. Box 300
Eilat, Israel 88102
972-7-334404
FAX: 972-7-333771

Lucky Divers
Red Sea Tower
Eilat, Israel
972-7-334706
FAX: 972-7-371057
Also operates the liveaboard *M/Y Suellyn*

Red Sea Surveyor
P.O. Box 552
Eilat, Israel 88104
972-7-335067
FAX: 972-7-335067
Operate liveaboard boat *Sea Surveyor*

Colour, Light and Water
P.O. Box 776
Eilat, Israel 88106
972-7-372267
FAX: 972-7-372267
Operate dive and sailboat *S/Y Poolster*

Colona Divers
Eilat, Israel
Operate liveaboard boats *Colona II and IV*

Fantasea Cruises
P.O. Box 234
Hofit, Israel 40295
972-53-666482
FAX: 972-53-663262
Operate liveaboard boat the *Fantasea II*

Sharm El Sheikh, Egypt

Land-based Operators:

Sinai Divers
At the Ghazala Hotel, Na'ama Bay
Sharm El Sheikh
2062-600150, 600151, 600158
FAX: 2062-600155, 600158
Contact: Rolf or Petra

Embarak Diving Resorts
Shark Bay
Sharm El Sheikh
2062-600208
FAX: 2062-600195

Sinai Dive Club
At the Fayrouz Hilton Hotel, Na'ama Bay
Sharm El Sheikh
2062-770788
FAX: 2062-776736

Aquanaute Diving Center
Na'ama Bay
Sharm El Sheikh
2062-600619
FAX: 2062-600619

Red Sea Diving College
Na'ama Bay
Sharm El Sheikh
2062-600145
FAX: 2062-600144

Colona Dive Club
At the Kanabesh Village, Na'ama Bay
Sharm El Sheikh
2062-600184, 600185
FAX: 2062-600185

Aquamarine International Diving Club
At the Aquamarine Hotel, Na'ama Bay
Sharm El Sheikh
2062-600176
FAX: 2062-600276

Camel Dive Club
Na'ama Bay
Sharm El Sheikh
2062-600700
FAX: 2062-600601

Dolphin Beach Resort
Dolphin Beach near Neweiba
Sinai, Egypt
202-576963, 5746943
FAX: 202-762298

Subex Diving Center
At the Moevenpick Hotel, Na'ama Bay
Sharm El Sheikh
Contact Moevenpick International Reservations

Tiran Dive Club
At the Tiran Hotel, Na'ama Bay
Sharm El Sheikh
2062-600285
FAX: 2062-600285

Red Sea Diving Center
At the Helnan Hotel, Na'ama Bay
Sharm El Sheikh

Liveaboard Operators:

Sinai Divers
At the Ghazala Hotel, Na'ama Bay
Sharm El Sheikh
2062-600150, 600151, 600158
FAX: 2062-600155, 600158
Operate the *Ghazala I* and the *Ghazala II*

Sea Divers
18 El-Sheikh Moh'd Abdalla Draz
Heliopolis
Cairo, Egypt
202-660515
FAX: 202-2907828
Operate the *Perla I* and the *Perla II*

Ram Cruise Lines
15 Shahid Galal Hagag Street
Heliopolis
Cairo, Egypt
202-2907509
FAX: Same
Operate the Crissy II

Luxury Dive Charters Ltd.
Whitefield Road
Bredbury, Stockport
Cheshire SK6 255
England
44-61-430-6818
FAX: 44-61-430-7920
Operate the *Poseidon's Quest*

Explorer Ventures USA Ltd.
10 Fencerow Drive
Fairfield, CT 06430-7001
U.S.A.
800-322-3577
FAX: 203-259-9896
Operate the *M/S Number One*

◀ *A colorful goatfish is typical on the reefs throughout the Red Sea.*

Hilton International Resorts Worldwide
Red Sea Cruise Desk
C/O Sharm El Sheikh Fayrouz Hilton Village
Sharm El Sheikh
2062-600136, 600137, 600138, 600139
FAX: 2062-770726
Operate the *M/V Gaia* and the *M/V Cybele*

Red Sea Travel Specialists

Adventure Express Travel
650 Fifth Street, Suite 505
San Francisco, CA 94107
U.S.A.
415-442-0799
FAX: 415-442-0289

See & Sea Travel Service, Inc.
50 Francisco Street
San Francisco, CA 94133
U.S.A.
415-434-3400
FAX: 415-434-3409

Poseidon Adventures
359 San Miguel Dr.
Newport Beach, CA 92660
1-800-854-9334
In Houston:
505 N. Belt, Suite 275
Houston, Texas 77060
713-820-DIVE

Tropical Adventures Travel
800-247-3483
In Wash. 206-441-3483
FAX: 206-441-5431

Underwater Photographic Specialists

Under Water Photo Center
At the Red Sea Diving College, Na'ama Bay
Sharm El Sheikh
2062-600145
FAX: 2062-600144
Photographic and videographic rentals, sales

Dusk at a night mooring. About to prepare for a night dive, this liveaboard diveboat enjoys the best the Red Sea has to offer. (Photo: Robert Stribling)

Index